S0-ACZ-485

Fossilized!
HUMAN FOSSILS

By Kathleen Connors

Gareth Stevens
Publishing

Please visit our website, www.garethstevens.com. For a free color catalog of all our high-quality books, call toll free 1-800-542-2595 or fax 1-877-542-2596.

Library of Congress Cataloging-in-Publication Data

Connors, Kathleen.
Human fossils / Kathleen Connors.
    p. cm.— (Fossilized!)
Includes index.
ISBN 978-1-4339-6414-5 (pbk.)
ISBN 978-1-4339-6415-2 (6-pack)
ISBN 978-1-4339-6412-1 (library binding)
1. Fossil hominids—Juvenile literature. I. Title.
GN282.C592 2012
569.9—dc23

                                    2011019785

First Edition

Published in 2013 by
Gareth Stevens Publishing
111 East 14th Street, Suite 349
New York, NY 10003

Copyright © 2013 Gareth Stevens Publishing

Designer: Katelyn E. Reynolds
Editor: Kristen Rajczak

Photo credits: Cover, pp. 1, 6–7, 8, (cover, pp. 1, 3–24 background and graphics) Shutterstock.com; p. Photos.com/ Thinkstock; p. 5 Lynn Johnson/National Geographic/Getty Images; pp. 9, 11, 16–17 Kenneth Garrett/National Geographic/ Getty Images; p. 12 Prehistoric/The Bridgeman Art Library/Getty Images; p. 13 Robert F. Sisson/National Geographic/Getty Images; p. 15 Dave Einsel/Getty Images; p. 16 iStockphoto/Thinkstock; p. 18 Dorling Kindersley/The Agency Collection/ Getty Images; p. 19 Hemera/Thinkstock; p. 20 Lillian Omariba/AFP/Getty Images; p. 21 Mario Tama/Getty Images.

Printed in the United States of America

CPSIA compliance information: Batch #CW12GS: For further information contact Gareth Stevens, New York, New York at 1-800-542-2595.

CONTENTS

Words in the glossary appear in **bold** type the first time they are used in the text.

STUDYING FOSSILS

Have you ever heard that humans and apes have a common **ancestor**? During the late 1800s, a scientist named Charles Darwin wrote about this ancestor in a book about human **evolution**.

Many scientists today still think apes and humans were linked in the past. However, **paleoanthropologists** have learned a lot more about ancient humans since Darwin's book came out. Much of what they know has come from studying fossils, which are remains or marks of plants and animals that formed over thousands or millions of years.

◀ Charles Darwin

THE FOSSIL RECORD

Paleoanthropology is the study of early humans. It's a combination of anthropology—the study of humans—and paleontology—the study of fossils.

Even small pieces of fossilized bone like these can help scientists learn about the past.

FOSSILIZED BONES

Most of the fossils paleoanthropologists study are parts of ancient human **skeletons**. Fossils formed when the bones turned to stone. The living parts of the bones broke down, and the nonliving parts filled with **minerals** through tiny openings called pores.

Fossilized bones help scientists learn about the way the human body changed over millions of years. Sometimes, human fossils are found near plant or animal fossils. These may be able to show how ancient humans died or what their last meal was!

THE FOSSIL RECORD

Some fossilized bones are found near simple tools or other **artifacts**.

Many times, fossilized bones belonging to the same skeleton are found near each other.
▽

EARLY FINDS

In 1857, part of a **skull** was found in Germany. It was very thick. No one was sure how old it was or if it was even human! Similar fossils were found in Belgium in 1886. Scientists later decided these fossils were from a group of very early humans, which they called Neanderthals.

During the late 1800s and early 1900s, more discoveries were made. Eugene Dubois uncovered the first fossils of another human **species** in Indonesia. It was called *Homo erectus*.

This Neanderthal skull looks different from a modern human skull.

THE FOSSIL RECORD

Since Dubois's find became known as *Homo erectus*, scientists have found 20 different human species! Modern humans are called *Homo sapiens*.

This *Homo erectus* skull was found at a famous human fossil site called Dmanisi in the Republic of Georgia.

9

DATING FOSSILS

The oldest fossils of humans and human ancestors date back about 4 to 6 million years. Many of the earliest of these fossils were found in Africa. Fossils of modern humans are between 100,000 and 200,000 years old.

There are a few ways for scientists to figure out how old a fossil is. They may use **superposition**. This establishes the fossil's age based on the rock layer it's found in. Radiometric dating is another method of measuring how old something is.

THE FOSSIL RECORD

Scientists don't always find fossils that can be studied. Sometimes, they don't have enough of the skeleton to study or the fossils are in poor condition.

Scientists spend many years putting broken
fossils together in order to study them.
▼

HOMINIDS

Humans and apes are part of the animal family Hominidae. Members of this family are called hominids. Ancient hominid fossils show some human features and some ape features. However, scientists don't always agree about the connection between these fossils, modern humans, and apes.

Paleoanthropologists have concluded that many human species and other hominids lived at the same time. Some scientists think animals such as lemurs are also part of the human family tree!

This drawing of a hominid called *Paranthropus boisei* shows what it might have looked like. ▶

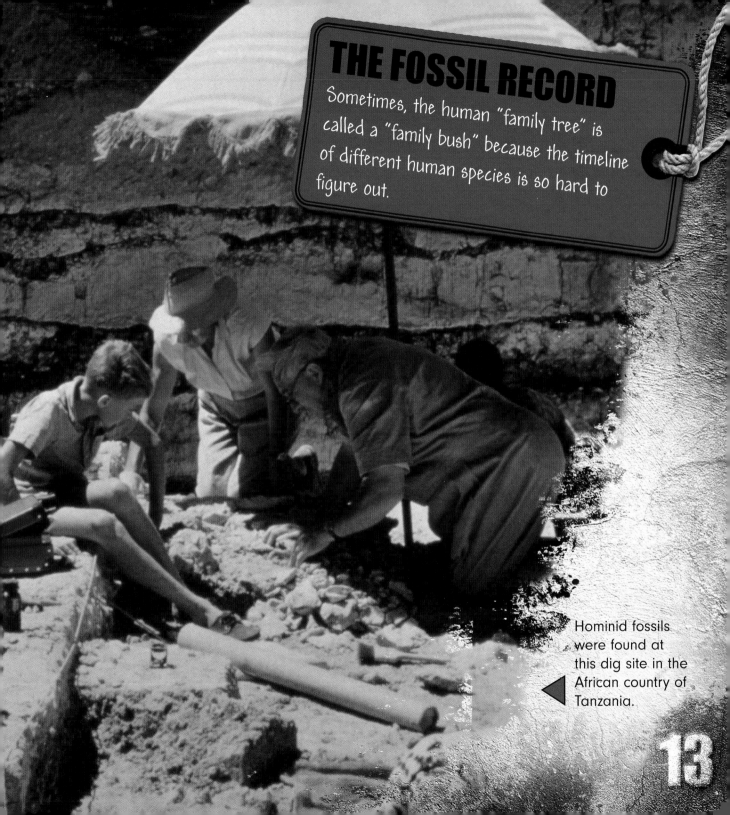

THE FOSSIL RECORD

Sometimes, the human "family tree" is called a "family bush" because the timeline of different human species is so hard to figure out.

Hominid fossils were found at this dig site in the African country of Tanzania.

FAMOUS FINDS

Scientists have found fossils from more than 6,000 individual humans or human ancestors. In 1974, a 3.4-million-year-old fossilized skeleton was found in Ethiopia. Scientists named it "Lucy." Lucy was the oldest and most complete skeleton of a human ancestor ever found at the time.

"Ardi" was found in Africa in 1992. In 2009, scientists first presented the 4.4-million-year-old skeleton. The fossilized skeleton of a **primate** called "Ida" was also presented in 2009. It taught scientists more about the connection between humans and apes.

THE FOSSIL RECORD

Ida was named after the young daughter of a scientist who studied the fossils.

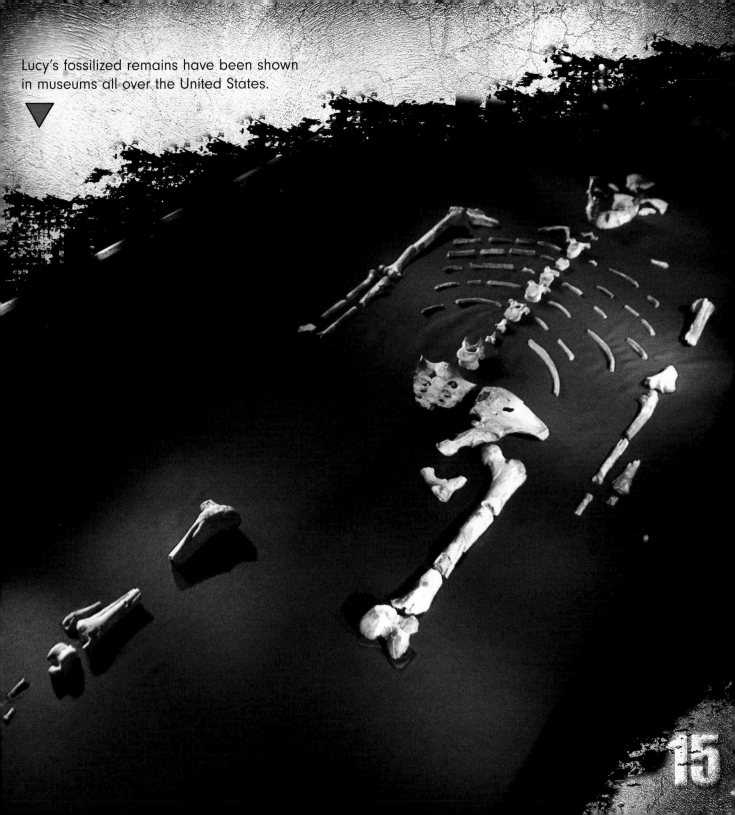

Lucy's fossilized remains have been shown in museums all over the United States.
▼

FOSSIL CLUES

Lucy, Ardi, Ida, and other fossils can tell us a lot about our human ancestors. Matter in the bones might offer clues about what the primates ate and the **climate** they lived in. By studying leg bones, scientists can figure out whether the primates spent more time in trees or on the ground.

Fossilized teeth can tell about the diets of human ancestors and ancient humans. More than 145 teeth were collected near where Ardi was found. Their wear patterns show that the group ate plants, nuts, and small animals.

Scientists can learn how evolved an ancient human was by the size and shape of its teeth.

16

THE FOSSIL RECORD

Many areas' climates have changed over millions of years. Plant and animal fossils help scientists discover what the conditions were once like.

Paleoanthropologists carefully remove fossils from the ground. They don't want to harm them.

BIPEDALISM

Modern humans are bipedal, or able to walk upright on two feet. However, paleoanthropologists have learned that some hominids and early humans walked on the ground, but used both their hands and feet to move through the trees.

The shape of a fossilized leg, hand, or pelvis—a large bone that connects the lower back and hips—shows how hominids and early humans moved around. Scientists cannot agree on whether our ancestors walked using their knuckles, like apes, at some point in time.

This picture shows how some people think modern humans evolved from ancient hominids.

Every time you see someone walking,
you are seeing bipedalism in action!

▼

ALWAYS CHANGING

Paleoanthropologists still have many questions about how humans evolved. When fossils are found, they're carefully studied. Sometimes it takes several years to clean the fossils enough to figure out if they're even human!

New finds can change what scientists think happened in the distant past. There are also many new ways to find out more about fossils that were found many years ago.

We can learn so much about our past from human fossils!

This fossil collection shows many hominid and early human skulls.

HUMAN FOSSIL FACTS

- By studying Ardi's skeleton, scientists discovered that Ardi was an adult female who was about 4 feet (1.2 m) tall and weighed 120 pounds (54 kg).

- A fossil called the "Piltdown Man" was found in 1912. However, in 1953, scientists discovered it was fake! A pair of paleontologists had connected an orangutan's jaw to a human's skull.

- Human ancestors didn't just leave behind bones. Ancient footprints have been found, too. These are called trace fossils.

- Ida's official name is Darwinius masillae. The skeleton was named in honor of Charles Darwin's 200th birthday.

GLOSSARY

ancestor: an animal that lived before others in its family tree

artifact: something made by humans in the past

climate: the weather conditions of a place over a period of time

evolution: the process of changes in a living thing that take place over many lifetimes

mineral: matter found in nature that is not living

paleoanthropologist: a person whose job it is to study early humans through their fossils

primate: any animal from the group that includes humans, apes, and monkeys

skeleton: the boney frame of the body

skull: the boney frame of the head and face

species: a group of animals that are all of the same kind

superposition: the placement of layers of rock on top of one another. The lower layers are older than the higher layers.

FOR MORE INFORMATION

Books

Croy, Anita. *Exploring the Past.* New York, NY: Marshall Cavendish Benchmark, 2011.

Dixon, Dougal. *Prehistoric World.* Tunbridge Wells, England: Ticktock Media, 2010.

Raham, Gary. *Fossils.* New York, NY: Chelsea House, 2008.

Websites

Human Evolution: You Try It
www.pbs.org/wgbh/aso/tryit/evolution/#
Read more about human evolution and do an activity.

Natural History Museum: Paleontologist
www.nhm.ac.uk/kids-only/ologist/palaeontologist/
Learn about a real paleontologist and how you can study fossils.

INDEX